THE JUDICIARY AND

JIMAI MONTIEL CALLES

THE JUDICIARY AND THE VENEZUELAN STATE

PROPOSALS FOR ITS STRENGTHENING BASED ON THE STRATEGIC PLAN 2013-2019

ScienciaScripts

This book is a translation from the original published under ISBN 978-613-8-97970-8.

Publisher:
Sciencia Scripts
is a trademark of
Dodo Books Indian Ocean Ltd. and OmniScriptum S.R.L publishing group

120 High Road, East Finchley, London, N2 9ED, United Kingdom
Str. Armeneasca 28/1, office 1, Chisinau MD-2012, Republic of Moldova, Europe

ISBN: 978-620-7-27232-7

SUMMARY

For decades, Venezuela has been characterised by its dynamic and oscillating economy, which has gone through various strategic plans aimed at sustaining and slowing down its influx and reducing the social impact it has generated. Similarly, procedures have been implemented aimed at strengthening the democratic and social rule of law and justice, as is the case of the Strategic Plan of the Judiciary 2013-2019, which is made up of five axes:

Management and Administration of the Judiciary: Renew the structures and processes of the Judiciary to raise the levels of effectiveness and efficiency, guaranteeing equal access to the administration of justice in the framework of the process of refounding the Republic;

New Public Servant of the Judiciary: to promote the training of the new public servant of the Judiciary, to guide his or her actions with a participatory and proactive, multi-ethnic and multicultural vision that contributes to guaranteeing the legality of administrative actions and effective judicial protection;

Strengthen social participation: Deepen social participation in the actions of the bodies that make up the Judiciary and in the administration of justice as an expression of popular sovereignty, contributing to increasing the culture of law and peace in the population;

Promote strategies to improve the quality of life of the communities by radiating the environment of the headquarters of the Judiciary through the Point and Circle Policy; and

International legal integration: To broaden the participation of the Judiciary in the international arena for the defence of sovereignty, self-determination and the definitive emancipation of the peoples, aimed at contributing to the process of integration of Our America, the construction of a pluricentric, multipolar world and the globalisation of justice in general.

These plans enshrine as a cornerstone general political, social, economic, legal and technological dimensions, in compliance with the theoretical requirements The fact that, at the level of external exercise, strictly speaking, it does not imply an instantaneous improvement.

The judicial system in Venezuela deserves to broaden its tactics and implement a monitoring and evaluation model to improve the management of the Strategic Plan of the Judiciary, with an integral vision of the critical knots at the cognitive, political, cultural, participatory, and transformational levels of the old structures, based on Strategic Planning and new forms of effective government. I therefore propose to review the paradigm of Open Justice for its implementation in the country as a way of discussing and executing public policies based on evidence that will improve the results achieved, increase levels of trust and improve the relationship between justice and society. It should be noted that it is not enough to identify the problem and generate a theoretical framework to counteract it; a thorough monitoring of this is required to be able to give concise answers to the needs on which the plan was based, being the only evidence of the prosperity or otherwise of the executed process. This lack of effective and continuous monitoring can lead to the decline of the proposal and its failure.

CONTENTS

INTRODUCTION

For almost two decades, the Venezuelan judiciary has been immersed in a process of change and transformation in its environment in accordance with constitutional principles and national plans for economic and social development. For this reason, the system's institutions have implemented a long-term plan that goes beyond the objectives and actions carried out through the annual institutional operational plan, which only made possible the ordinary functioning of the judiciary for a period of one year.

The first step for implementation was to draw up the proposal, complemented by the contributions of the social dialogue carried out during the years 2013-2014, generating a series of recommendations at that time, by the various actors such as workers, social movements, among others, for the improvement of the Judiciary. Likewise, the information provided by the Social Observatory of the Judiciary made it possible to outline the changes expected in this branch of the national public power.

The second step was the implementation of the Judicial Branch Strategic Plan 2013-2019, in the quest to consolidate a democratic and social State based on the rule of law and justice. The purpose of this paper is to analyse the implementation of the strategic lines of action, in its strategic axis 1: Management and Administration of the Judiciary, making it possible to verify the scope of the purposes with the execution in order to recommend new lines of action if necessary.

In any case, any strategic plan should be considered a document subject to revisions and/or modifications, in virtue of the multiple variants that occur during its implementation, for example, when the objectives outlined in the 2013-2019 timeframe are no longer valid, when the incorporation of others may be necessary to face the changing environment, or when the actions are not possible or are not adjusted in time and economic effort.

In this sense, this work is structured in the first phase, with the presentation and justification, describing the problem, the purposes and the relevance of the study. In the following phases, the theoretical and methodological considerations for the evaluation of the Strategic Plan of the Judiciary are presented, ending with the results and the proposal.

1. PRESENTATION AND SUBSTANTIATION OF THE STUDY

1.1. Approaches to the Socio-Political Context of the Problem

With the exhaustion of the neoliberal model at the end of the 20th century, the debate on the need to rebuild its management capacity began to take shape in most Latin American states. For this reason, Vilas (2011) argues that the reorientation of the state in response to the economic, social and political crisis at the end of the last century and the beginning of the present in Latin American countries such as Argentina, Bolivia, Ecuador and Venezuela, the latter being the particular case of this study, allows us to discern new paradigms for the production and implementation of public policies.

In this context, important countries of the continent have glimpsed their commitment to the social transformation of state leadership, emphasising the public agenda and implementation of policies with social impact on the most disadvantaged populations and those with fewer opportunities. In the American continent, the social, political and economic situation in the first and second decade of the 20th century highlighted the accentuation of poverty from 2015 to 2019 before the pandemic, according to data from the Economic Commission for Latin America and the Caribbean (ECLAC); when 30.1% of the region's population was below the poverty line in 2018, while 10.7% lived in extreme poverty, rates that increased to 30.8% and 11.5% respectively in 2019, these indicators could be evidence of the inability of public management to address the reality described.

In relation to the strengthening of democracies in Latin America, this implies, among other challenges, building governments and institutions capable of resolving priority problems in a plural and politically competitive public space. It also requires that public policies transcend their role as a technical instrument, and that their design respond to real, unresolved situations that are intended to be solved, implemented efficiently with an evaluation and follow-up plan (Arellano, 2014).

It should be pointed out that Latin American countries with significant reforms in their state apparatus, and profound transformations in their public policies, still present weaknesses in their planning, management and evaluation capacity, opening gaps for ineffectiveness and inefficiency in state institutions. In this sense, the new public intervention is not only legitimised by effectiveness and transparency, it also requires a The need to establish evaluation and monitoring as a strategy for updating and reviewing results on an on-going basis. With the entry into force of the Constitution of the Bolivarian Republic of Venezuela (1999), a range of opportunities opened up for participation in the country, defining the democratic condition as participatory and protagonist, implying the co-participation of citizens in the formulation of public policies, This also demands the transformation of the State and its institutions, which is why it is pertinent to analyse the strategic guidelines proposed by the Judiciary during 2013-2019 in order to redefine the new orientations after their implementation.

An unresolved and worrying problem in the development of democracies and the quality of their public management is the lack of periodic evaluations in the implementation of public policies, a common denominator in the countries of the continent, of which Venezuela is no exception, and for this reason it is necessary to have a methodology for monitoring that allows information to be obtained on the results of the objectives and strategies planned over time, making the pertinent adjustments according to the new scenarios.In the case of Venezuela, during the government of President Hugo Rafael Chavez Frfas, a whole bureaucratic apparatus was configured around the creation and execution of public policies to tackle the country's main social problems, such as education, health, poverty and inequality, which was maintained during his two terms in office (1999-2006, 2007-2012). It is worth noting that most of these policies were presented under an organisational scheme called missions, many of which are still in force today.

In most of the public policies designed and implemented during the government of President Chavez, a high impact on the existing problems can be observed, as well as an integral and positive approach. However, in the specific issue of the judiciary, having certainty in quantitative terms has not been easy, due to the lack of follow-up, monitoring and evaluation of the policies developed, which presupposes a lack of planning for the subsequent control of these policies. With regard to the evaluation experience of the proposed Strategic Plan of the Judiciary, it is important to highlight its sui generis nature, since it is anchored for the first time to the General Plan for the Economic Development of the Nation called "Plan de la Patria" (Plan for the Homeland) for the same period (2013-2019), a very significant advance for public management and the search for institutional transformation based on the planning system, implying a high commitment for the Venezuelan State, the monitoring and visibility of the results achieved.

In this sense, with the aim of validating previous knowledge in the field of public management and systematising the institutional reality of the Venezuelan State in relation to the judiciary as a branch of the National Public Power, the study asks the following question: What is the perception of the implementation of the strategic plan of the judiciary in Venezuela for the period 2013-2019, in relation to axis 1: management and administration?

1.2. General research purposes:

Analyse the implementation of the strategic plan of the judiciary in Venezuela for the period 2013-2019 with emphasis on the management and administration axis.

Specific:

1. Describe the socio-political context of evaluation and monitoring of the strategic plan of the judiciary in Venezuela.
2. To characterise the management of the judiciary in Venezuela from the perspective of the actors involved in the Strategic Plan, highlighting subjective elements immersed in the process and organisation.
3. Identify the structures of democratic, participatory relations established in the judiciary's strategic plan with an impact on the quality of its management.
4. Establish theoretical and methodological contributions on the evaluation of the strategic plan of the judiciary in Venezuela.
5. Interpret guidelines to strengthen the judiciary and the Venezuelan state on the basis of the 2013-2019 strategic plan.

1.3. Relevance of the research

According to the World Bank report (1993), governance implies the way in which power is exercised in the management of economic and social resources for development, referring of course to the power of governments when defining and resolving public policies. However, over time, technocrats (specialists) have been busy formulating methods to develop public policies in an effective way, delivering to governments ideal projects in different fields, which for multiple reasons are not executed as they were initially thought, placing public management at risk of ineffectiveness due to their inadequate intervention. This happens when those in charge of designing government strategies are not the same people who are present in the implementation process, let alone in the monitoring and evaluation. Hence the importance of giving evaluation its leading role in the life cycle of public policies, which is why this study is important in contributing to the construction of knowledge on the design of evaluations with the possibility of influencing decision-making in institutional management.From a practical and social point of view, the proposed analysis constitutes a reflective contribution, which will awaken the interest of the different social actors, including authorities, civil servants and other members of the judicial government, in evaluation as a management tool that is scarcely applied in the areas where it is necessary to concentrate efforts in order to achieve long-term strategic objectives; therefore, it is opportune to produce knowledge about the ways of evaluating. Specifically, the Venezuelan Judiciary needs to adapt to social, economic, and political changes, new information technologies, virtual environments due to the recent pandemic experienced by the world, institutions need to renew and respond to these new demands of society, in this sense, the evaluation of the strategic plan 2013-2019, is relevant and consistent with the needs raised. Therefore, its theoretical contribution to the understanding and theorisation of public policy and its processes is considered relevant, and it also becomes a support for other studies related to the field of public management and democratic transformation.

2. FOUNDATIONS OF POLITICAL KNOWLEDGE, DEMOCRACY AND PUBLIC POLICY

For Cansino (2004), innovating political knowledge involves observing democracy as the result of social interaction and not only as a form of government, seeking to unveil the web of relationships and experiences surrounding the experience of citizens. The first is oriented towards theoretical production and positivist scientific research, defined by Sartori (1992) as the discipline based on the methodology of the empirical sciences to explain the various aspects of political reality. The second: focused on the complex and changing reality that emerges as a result of social demands (Cansino, 2004). In particular, this study focuses on the political knowledge of complexity, defined by Cansino (2008) as the object of study oriented by the complex and changing reality that involves not only institutions, but also subjects, actions, meanings, symbols and significations. For this author, in the political sphere, meanings are transmitted through a cumulus of signs, among which narratives and languages could be highlighted. In this axis of thought, political science defines its object of study on the basis of the multiple theoretical and methodological perspectives, in which the concept and/or the category is constructed, on the logic of whose internal movement depends the place occupied by the social interpretations of the phenomena of human coexistence.

According to this conception, democracy is studied as a symbolic device, i.e. a collective historical invention with full awareness of its existence; This perspective is oriented towards rethinking democracy and institutionality from its bases, that is to say, from the social subject or citizen, in the particular case of the object of study analysed, In the particular case of the object of study analysed, it will be to evaluate the

11

implementation of a specific issue of judicial policy in the period 2013-2019, based on the meanings given by the actors involved, which imprint their own symbols on judicial management in order to deconstruct and construct new reflexive knowledge of the process.

In relation to public policy, defined by Oszlak and O'Donnell (1981) as the set of actions and omissions that manifest a particular form of state intervention in response to a demanding issue of interest or the mobilisation of other civil society actors. These state interventions are characterised by the normative orientation that defines the state, i.e., the state's direction to meet the demands identified as primordial. In this way, public action becomes political, by virtue of the factors that determine its origin, adaptation or effectiveness, which lie mainly in the interaction between the different political, economic and social actors operating within and outside the state. According to Laswell (1962), policy design is structured by identifiable stages that can be analysed in isolation, among which are: the detection of the problem and needs; diagnosis and definition of the problem to be addressed; incorporation of the problem into the public agenda; design of the action plan; implementation and evaluation of the programme applied. In this planning process, evaluation is located in the final stage, since its purpose is to assess the results of the policy on the one hand and, on the other, to serve as a basis for continuing with the planning of public intervention over time through its feedback role. As foreseen with the analysis of the strategic plan of the judiciary, 2013-2019, by validating its effectiveness it will be possible to determine whether it is possible to continue or modify the initial approaches.

2.1. Public Policy Evaluation.

Following the epistemic route of the complexity of knowledge and in accordance with the purpose of analysing the implementation of the strategic plan of the Judiciary in Venezuela, 2013-2019 in relation to axis 1: management and administration. It is proposed to apply the evaluation, under the consideration of the results achieved by the strategic objectives, with a view to generating valuable information to improve the initially proposed guidelines, estimating its timeless condition is observed as a type of Ex-post evaluation.

According to the review of relevant methods and compared to what is expected to be achieved at the end of this analysis, the results-based approach to evaluation is considered. Precisely, Wholey (1983), quoted by Osuna & Marquez (2004); defines evaluation as a response to the demand of government representatives to evaluate their programmes with the objective of finding better ways to manage them, in the criteria of evaluation should be the basis for improving management, making the performance and results of the programmes administered visible.

In this initial discussion phase, it is possible to incorporate another approach to complement the research and understanding of the process, based on interaction with the subjects involved through interviews, outlined according to the defined objectives. Considering that evaluation should not be conceived as an isolated and definitive event, but rather as a continuous process during the planning, implementation and evaluation stages in order to strengthen administrative management through the timely detection of unresolved problems.

2.2. Configuraci6n del Poder Público en la Constituci6n de la República Bolivariana de Venezuela de 1999.

In accordance with Article 136 of the Constitution, the National Public Power is divided into Legislative, Executive, Judicial, Citizen and Electoral branches. Each of the branches has its own functions, with the bodies responsible for their exercise collaborating with each other in the achievement of the purposes of the State.

The Judiciary, according to the National Constitution, possesses autonomy by defining itself as independent, with the Supreme Court enjoying functional, financial and administrative autonomy. Its functioning is based on two per cent of the ordinary national budget, which may not be reduced or modified without the prior authorisation of the National Assembly. The Supreme Court of Justice is responsible for the government, administration and direction of the judiciary, including the preparation and execution of its ordinary budget. (Articles 254 and 267).

2.2.1. Description of the Strategic Plan of the Venezuelan Judiciary 2013-2019.

"Consolidating a Democratic and Social State of Law and Justice". Taking

The judiciary, in order to create the conditions for its transformation, is developing the strategic guidelines for the period 2013-2019, responding to the need to develop a long-term plan that goes beyond the objectives and actions implemented in the Plan of the Homeland (2013-2019). In order to generate the conditions that make its transformation possible, the judiciary is developing strategic guidelines for the period 2013-2019, responding to the need to develop a long-term plan that exceeds the objectives and actions implemented through the institutional annual operational plan. In this sense, five axes and strategic lines of action of the Judiciary were identified:

Strategic line I Management and Administration of the Judiciary

Renew the structures and processes of the judiciary to raise the levels of effectiveness and efficiency, guaranteeing equal access to the administration of justice in the framework of the process of refounding the Republic.

Strategic line II New Public Servant of the Judiciary

Promote the training of the new public servant of the Judiciary, in order to guide his or her actions with a participatory and proactive, multi-ethnic and multicultural vision that contributes to guaranteeing the legality of administrative actions and effective judicial protection.

Strategic axis III Strengthening social participation.

Deepen social participation in the actions of the bodies that make up the Judicial Branch and in the administration of justice as an expression of popular sovereignty, contributing to increasing the legal and peace culture in the population.

Strategic axis IV Policy of the dot and circle to promote the good life

Promote strategies to improve the quality of life of the communities by radiating the environment of the headquarters of the Judiciary through the "dot and circle" policy.

Strategic thrust V International legal integration

To broaden the participation of the Judiciary in the international arena for the defence of sovereignty, self-determination and the definitive emancipation of the peoples, aimed at contributing to the process of integration of Our America, the construction of a pluricentric, multipolar world and the globalisation of justice in general.

Table 1: Object of Study

Strategic Line of Action 1: MANAGEMENT AND ADMINISTRATION OF THE JUDICIAL POWERS

Strategic Line 1: Renew the structures and processes of the Judiciary to raise the levels of effectiveness and efficiency, guaranteeing equal access to the administration of justice within the framework of the process of refounding the Republic.	
Strategic Objectives	Strategic Actions
1. Optimise the conditions to guarantee access to justice, effective judicial protection and due process for the protection of national and collective interests, as well as to enhance the dignity and development of the personality in a democratic, participatory and protagonist society.	Strengthen the strategic planning and coordination bodies of the Justice System to unify policies that guarantee access to justice, procedural speed, effective judicial protection and the development of alternative means of justice within the framework of Article 253 of the CRBV. Implement a plan for the growth, refurbishment, redistribution and reallocation of the infrastructure of judicial headquarters aimed at raising the quality of service at all levels of the judiciary, combating congestion and improving health, working conditions and the working environment. Implement a plan to optimise the workforce as a transformative social process in accordance with its technical capacities, skills, experience and academic training aimed at raising the levels of effectiveness and efficiency of the judiciary. Review and update the manuals of rules and procedures in accordance with the process of transformation of the structures and management of the judiciary. Deconcentrate the structure and management of the judiciary on the basis of a new national geopolitics that responds to the processes of community organisation and aggregation. Advance towards a comprehensive security system for the protection of jurisdictional activity and the integrity of users and public servants of the Judiciary to be implemented throughout the national territory. Implement protocol policies in all Judicial Branch headquarters that transform

	the security patrol for access and permanence in the facilities into a cordial process of reception, orientation and adequate attention to all users as part of a comprehensive security policy. Strengthen the technological infrastructure to interconnect all the headquarters of the Judiciary to enable the implementation of integrated information systems. Strengthen the tools and computer systems that facilitate the registration, streamlining, coordination and transparency of judicial processes, allowing the verification of the concurrence or relationship between different cases in the different jurisdictions. 1.10. Create the new single statistical system of the Judiciary. Implement a plan for the provision of office material, furniture and technological equipment in accordance with the particular needs and requirements of each headquarters, giving priority to public sector bodies and entities or to national investment. Create the project for the digitisation of documents and electronic signature for the decongestion of physical archives. Consolidate procedural orality in all matters and strengthen audiovisual recording mechanisms in order to effectively dispense with unnecessary written records. Strengthen the ongoing monitoring and evaluation of the compliance with the planning and goals set with due inspection and control of works and projects in execution.
	Assume constitutional responsibility for the inspection and oversight of public defender's offices (Art. 267 of the CRBV). Reaffirm the role of the judge as the director of the judicial process by setting an example and guiding all actors and parties involved in the process. Promote multidisciplinarity and transdisciplinarity in the management teams of the Judiciary. Generate conditions and mechanisms to realise procedural equality and material justice in the face of the economic, cultural, political and communicational inequalities of the parties in conflict.

2. Strengthen and expand the bodies for receiving and processing complaints, as well as the offices for assistance, orientation and social participation, in order to facilitate access to services throughout the national territory.	Create regional offices of citizen attention and participation and of the Inspector General of Courts in the national territory, as a coordinated deconcentrated system, in order to guarantee an expeditious, transparent and more accessible service to citizens for the reception and processing of their complaints.} Expand complaints mechanisms, enhancing them through the use of information and communication technologies (ICTs). 2.3. Provide users with the means to follow up on and know the status of their complaints or requests.
3. Promote the development of a new institutional institutional framework based on the spirit and experience of the social missions, aimed at strengthening free, speedy and timely response with an emphasis on attention to vulnerable sectors.	Strengthen policies of free and easy access to justice administration bodies. Implement social inclusion policies and socio-legal care programmes in the poorest areas and hard-to-reach communities. Promote the development of community and institutional practices, internships and socio-legal research processes for the development of theoretical and practical experiences that contribute to guaranteeing access to justice. Strengthen the socialist justice mission to underpin the accompaniment, protection and legal attention of the most vulnerable sectors of society, aimed at universalising access to justice. Contribute to the process of transformation and humanisation of the prison system.
4. Develop a cultural and communications policy for the constitutional justice model that strengthens the information processes of the judiciary, facilitating interaction and social dialogue on the Venezuelan justice administration system.	Create a body for strategic management and communication that coordinates, unifies and executes the communications policy of the Judiciary. Implement communication campaigns to raise awareness, provide orientation, training and information on the scope of action of the judiciary through the Bolivarian Communication and Information System (SIBCI), alternative and community media, and private communication companies. Promote research and national consultations to ascertain citizens' perceptions of the Venezuelan justice system. To promote the publication of bibliography and documentary material that contributes to the development of the new emancipatory juridical thought of Our America. 4.5 Encourage the exchange of knowledge, experiences and practices in the field of justice that contribute to the development of participation, respect and recognition of cultural diversity. Facilitate the exercise of whistleblowing and the systematisation of proposals for the improvement of the judicial function.

	Promote the reaffirmation of national identity and the recognition of cultural diversity in the field of justice. To contribute to the transformation of the professional ethics of lawyers and the revaluation of the judicial function of this profession.
5. Implement policies that have a direct impact on the well-being of the workers of the judiciary and their social environment.	Facilitate the organisational processes of the employees of all bodies and agencies of the Judiciary in accordance with the provisions of the applicable legal system. Promote the discussion and validity of collective bargaining that honours the rights of workers in order to satisfy their basic needs and dignify their material and spiritual conditions, guaranteeing equality for all. Promote labour improvements through comprehensive support for workers and their families, through the development of the Social Security system of the Judiciary, attending to their needs for health, food, education, housing, recreation, transport, and others.
6. Strengthen the development of the jurisprudence of the Bolivarian Doctrine and the model of social justice, strengthening national sovereignty and the guarantee of social, economic and cultural rights in balance with individual, civil and political rights, framed in the promotion of the just distribution of wealth and the supreme happiness of the people.	Promote the defence of national interests and the supreme happiness of the people by protecting the social process of work, the essential sources of wealth of Venezuelan society and strategic areas for national security. Protect the sovereignty and self-determination of the Venezuelan people against threats and aggressions, through the application and constitutional development of the Bolivarian doctrine. Continue to ensure the comprehensive security of the nation through judicial decisions. Promote the defence of environmental rights and the development of the rights of Mother Earth in order to preserve life on the planet and thus save the human species. Promote the rescue and jurisprudential development of the emancipatory legal thought of our peoples. Promote the full and integral guarantee of human rights with emphasis on the enforceability of collective and social rights in order to put them on a par with the protection of individual rights. Reaffirm the development of gender equality and protection of the rights of the sexually diverse population. Reaffirm the protection of workers as creators of the socially produced wealth, as protagonists of the education and work

	processes that are essential to guarantee the rights of the individual, the family and society as a whole.
	Promote the implementation of the laws of the people's power, which are fundamental norms for the development of participatory and protagonist democracy.
	6.1O. Promote the development of economic rights, centred on the fair distribution of wealth and the deployment of the values and principles of the socio-economic system established in the Bolivarian Constitution.
	Reaffirm the multi-ethnic and multicultural character of our society by recognising the rights of indigenous peoples and communities, and the multiple expressions of our cultural diversity.
	Propose the development of the Special Indigenous Jurisdiction and the Special Jurisdiction of Communal Justice of the Peace.

Taken from the Judicial Branch Strategic Plan 2013-2019, and adapted by Montiel (2023).

2.3. Democratisation of Justice

The recent global pandemic demonstrated the responsiveness of nation-states to social demands for the administration of justice, and exposed the weaknesses of democracies and their institutions, Particularly in Latin America, the justice system faces great challenges to consolidate democratic processes, with full independence of state powers and respect for the rule of law, so what seemed to be a threat to the institutional framework due to the obligatory social distancing, became an opportunity to transform management from within with a view to creating the conditions for effective judicial governance. According to the Justice Studies Centre of the Americas (JSCA), the recent discussion on judicial governance inevitably brings with it a focus on politics and the independence of the judge vis-à-vis the rest of the public authorities and interest groups. Considering fundamentally the operational dimension of the organisation and the actions of judges within the framework of their functional autonomy, the failure to distinguish between the political and administrative functions in the judiciary, especially those exercised by senior officials, is leading to a lack of understanding by society of the dynamics of justice on the one hand and, on the other, to questioning among members of the judiciary about the processes of transparency, management of the system and impartiality. In this regard, Binder (2006) argues that the weak independence of judges in Latin America has been a structural problem since the establishment of democracies in the continent, affecting the ability of judges to comply with the law, administer justice inherent to the exercise of their function and control public power as a guarantor of impunity. At the same time, the vision of these conditions or burdens placed on judges has been superficially limited to the moral and ethical, with the current discussion focusing on overcoming this simplistic and reductionist vision of judicial government to one with a broader vision of the participatory and democratic principles of state institutions and the judiciary, This is where the definition of open justice emerges, implying a philosophy in the way justice is administered based on fundamental principles such as transparency, participation and collaboration-coworking. Therefore, thinking about the democratisation of justice involves reviewing the conditions and management capacities of judicial institutions, their relationship with the public, the impact of corruption on public confidence, and the relationship between the judiciary and citizens. processes of organisation, planning, evaluation, transparency, accountability, optimisation of resources and judicial efficiency. Precisely under these precepts, the intention to evaluate the implementation of the strategic plan of the Judiciary in Venezuela 2013-2019 is consolidated, in relation to its axis 1: management and administration.

21

3. ABOUT THE METHODOLOGICAL ROUTE

This study orients the search for new knowledge with a profound approach to the implementation of the Strategic Plan of the Judiciary in Venezuela 2013-2019, in its Management and Administration axis, considering the rational and logical epistemic matrix of subjectivity, in which the background is the existence and experience are the means to understand the perception of the subjects on the basis of their experience and thought. According to Taylor and Bodgan (1992), it represents a human group's own peculiar way of assigning meanings to things and events, i.e. in its capacity and way of symbolising. Under this argument, the route of complexity is traced as an approach to approach in a simple way the context and theorisation of the object of study.

3.1.1. Information Gathering Techniques

In order to provide real and concrete evidence of the implementation of the Strategic Plan described above, an instrument was designed to apply the interview technique to key informants in the institution, as well as participant and documentary observation respectively (see table 2).

Table 2: Techniques and tools

Techniques	Instruments	Resource
Observation Participant	Anecdotal records	Notebook
Interview a Key informants	Interview Gufa	Digital recorder
Focus Group	Group discussion	Chat Interactive

Montiel (2023)

3.1.2. Sample

Based on key informants, who were interviewed to gather information on the Strategic Plan, axis 1 on management, and selected according to the profile criteria outlined in table 3:

Table 3: Key informants

SUBJECTS	ACTOR	PERFIL
1	Authority	Leader in public management
1	Civil servant	Staff seconded to the authorities judicial
1	Interest Group	Trade union representative
1	Expert	Evaluation and monitoring

Montiel (2023)

4. ANALYSIS, INTERPRETATION AND THEORISING

4.1.First moment: Getting to know

On the conceptual basis of the historical objectives of the Economic and Social Development Plan, known as the Plan for the Homeland for the period 2013-2019. Interpretative matrix of the socio-political context of the Strategic Plan of the Judiciary

Specific Aim of the Study: To describe the socio-political context of evaluation and monitoring of the Strategic Plan of the Judiciary.	
Focus: RBV Constitution (1999) Social State of Law, Justice and Equity. Lineas Generales del Plan de la Patria 2013-2019, (Defend, expand and consolidate national independence; construction of Bolivarian socialism of the 20th century; convert Venezuela into a powerful country; contribute to the development of a new international geopolitics; preserve life on the planet and the human species.	
Social policy from the National Plan 2013-2019	Social policy from the Strategic Plan of the Judiciary 2013-2019
National Objective 2.2.Building a just and egalitarian society Strategic Objectives 2.2.8.1. Combat impunity and procedural delays in coordination with the public authorities involved. 2.2.8.4..Transform the Criminal Justice System, generating alternatives for the serving of sentences, as well as other procedural benefits that help to reduce the number of sentences. to the shaping of a new order of administration 2.3. Consolidate and expand popular power and socialist democracy. To achieve full sovereignty as a major essential element of the Bolivarian project,	Strategic Line of Action 1: Management and Administration of the Judiciary Understood as the institutional configuration developed under the precepts of a new political culture within the framework of participatory and protagonist democracy. With a view to the democratisation of processes, optimisation of resources and transformation of public management.
2.3.1. Promote the construction of a social welfare state. Law and justice through the awareness and expansion of organised people's power.	

Prepared by Montiel (2013). For more information, see Plan de la Patria 2013- 2019. Segundo Plan de Desarrollo Econ6mico y Social de la Naci6n.

In the same vein, the strategic actions are illustrated on the basis of the theoretical and operational matrices of the first objective of the Strategic Plan of the Judiciary 2013-2019.

Matrix for Axis 1: Management and Administration of the Judiciary.

Strategic Line 1: Renew the structures and processes of the judiciary to raise the levels of effectiveness and efficiency, guaranteeing equal access to the administration of justice within the framework of the process of refounding the republic.
Objective: To optimise conditions to guarantee access to justice, effective judicial protection and due process for the protection of national and collective interests, as well as to enhance the dignity and development of the personality in a democratic, participatory and protagonist society. Strategic Actions: 18
Strengthen the strategic planning and coordination bodies of the Justice System to unify policies that guarantee access to justice, procedural speed, effective judicial protection and the development of alternative means of justice within the framework of Article 253 of the CRBV.
Implement a plan for the growth, refurbishment, redistribution and reallocation of the infrastructure of judicial headquarters aimed at raising the quality of service at all levels of the judiciary, combating congestion and improving health, working conditions and the working environment.
Implement a plan to optimise the workforce as a transformative social process in accordance with its technical capacities, skills, experience and academic training aimed at raising the levels of effectiveness and efficiency of the judiciary.
Review and update the manuals of rules and procedures in accordance with the process of transformation of the structures and management of the judiciary.
Deconcentrate the structure and management of the judiciary on the basis of a new national geopolitics that responds to the processes of community organisation and aggregation.
Advance towards a comprehensive security system for the protection of jurisdictional activity and the integrity of users and public servants of the Judiciary to be implemented throughout the national territory.
Implement protocol policies in all Judicial Branch headquarters that transform the security patrol for access and permanence in the facilities into a cordial process of reception, orientation and adequate attention to all users as part of a comprehensive security policy.
Strengthen the technological infrastructure to interconnect all the headquarters of the Judiciary to enable the implementation of integrated information systems.
Strengthen the tools and computer systems that facilitate the registration, streamlining, coordination and transparency of judicial processes, allowing the verification of the concurrence or relationship between different cases in the different jurisdictions.
1O. Create the new single statistical system of the Judiciary.
Implement a plan for the provision of office material, furniture and technological equipment in accordance with the particular needs and

requirements of each headquarters, giving priority to public sector bodies and entities or to national investment.
Set up the project for the digitisation of documents and electronic signatures to relieve congestion in the physical archives.
Consolidate procedural orality in all matters and strengthen audiovisual recording mechanisms in order to effectively dispense with unnecessary written records.
Strengthen the permanent monitoring and evaluation of the fulfilment of the planning and goals set with the due inspection and control of works and projects in execution.
15.Assume constitutional responsibility for the inspection and oversight of public defender's offices (Art. 267 of the CRBV).
16.Reaffirm the role of the judge as the director of the judicial process by setting an example and guiding all actors and parties involved in the process.
17.Promote multidisciplinarity and transdisciplinarity in the management teams of the Judiciary.
18.Generate conditions and mechanisms to realise procedural equality and material justice in the face of the economic, cultural, political and communicational inequalities of the parties in conflict.

Source: Strategic Plan of the Judiciary of the RBV. 2013-2019. Adapted from Montiel (2023).

Regarding this review of the Strategic Plan 2013-2019, related to the axis of Management and Administration, as a prior action to validate the relevance and consistency of its resolutions with the needs of the environment and to assess the conformity of its proposals with the guidelines of the National Economic and Social Development Plan of the country, based on the aspects of quality, relevance, internal and external coherence, it is interpreted that the Plan is consistent with the general environment, in its external dimensions such as: political, social, economic, legal, technological, as it complies with the levels of quality and relevance. However, in the discussion of the strategies of the Management Plan, the internal coherence is questionable, as it is based on a set of actions that do not necessarily imply or lead to change or improvement of the operational functioning of the judicial institution.

In addition, the operational matrices of the axis:Management and Administration of the Plan, synthesise 49 strategic actions, which have not had a significant transcendence for the achievement of the strategic objectives, which affects the achievement of the institution's constitutionally established aims and the general guidelines of the Nation, a situation which leads us to infer a lack of coordination between what is constitutionally established with the planning of the Nation and that of the Judiciary, According to the information provided by key informants, the process of implementing the strategies did not permeate the organisational structure or the information and control systems, generating a weak impact on the objectives set out in the management plan.

4.2. Moment Two: Doing

It involved organising the contents collected through the interviews and then categorising them, grouping them according to the thematic units, assigning meanings to the discourses, in accordance with the guidelines established in the data collection instruments.

Analysis matrix 1

Guidelines	Interviews	Subcategories Built	Expert assessment
	E1: There is little visibility of the actions that should have been carried out. There is not enough information about them (L:54- 57).	Consistency in monitoring and evaluation instruments	Judicial Officer: Implemented projects should be evaluated in the short to medium term.
The evaluation of the plan of the judiciary in Venezuela.	E2. The absence of strategic planning and coordination bodies is one of the current problems of the justice system, as the function to be performed by planning bodies has been carried out by judges and legal professionals, located at Posts with administrative functions.(L:94-99)	The function The evaluation function is carried out by professionals inexperienced in the area.	The existing existing evaluation are applied in a timeless manner.
	E3: Evaluation has been of little relevance because it is not monitored and controlled (L:26-28).	Ineffective implementation due to a lack of lack of Monitoring and control of action strategies.	Judicial Management policies can be made more effective by increasing the the Investment in technological endowment y an advisory body in the Planning Directorate
	E4: The importance given to evaluation has nothing to do with the purposes of management. Unfortunately, the evaluations that are carried out are often aimed at controlling the subjects, i.e. the officials, and not the processes that have to be reviewed by the respective coordination of planning on the objectives and goals established, i.e. performance. This is the negative aspect, as objectivity and the possibility of correcting what needs to be corrected in order to improve management is lost, which is what the judicial community expects so much from the judicial community. as well as civil society in receiving the judicial service.(E: 26-36)		

Prepared by Montiel (2023)

Evaluation as a category of analysis makes us contemplate the strategic actions implemented by the different bodies and dependencies of the judiciary, at the national, regional and municipal levels, in order to demonstrate the results obtained in the management process, whether they are effective or not. The important thing is to guide decision making in a timely manner in order to transform the given reality. In the observed judicial management, the strategic management process differs significantly from being conceptually and practically rigorous, leading to deficiencies in the design and implementation of strategies and projects, which negatively impacts on the scope of the general guidelines.

As the following accounts show: "...There has been no regular and periodic monitoring of the Strategic Plan by the Planning Directorate, nor have the communication mechanisms been generated that would allow me, as an official of the administration, to know the scope of the projects implemented, with timely information that would allow me to establish the pertinent corrective measures" (E3:L:28-36). Similarly, this opinion matrix is evidenced in the following testimony: "...The planning department of the TSJ should carry out monitoring and evaluation actions of the projects implemented by the management of the Strategic Plan. There is little visibility of the actions that should have been carried out, and there is insufficient information on them". (E1:L:51-56) In relation to the processes of control and monitoring of the jurisdictional function, the informant states that; "...a single system for monitoring cases has not been implemented, nor has a permanent system of statistics been set up to verify jurisdictional action and other indicators of national and international relevance, and there is no evidence of the necessary investment to cover the requirements and needs of the Courts" (E1:L:38-45)Comparing the testimonies with the documentary information of the Strategic Plan, it is observed that it does not include important elements for its effective implementation, such as: the analysis of the resources required for its execution, the assignment of responsibilities for the goals and objectives, the follow-up, revision and annual adjustment of its strategies, as well as the capacity for monitoring by indicators subject to the constant flow of information based on the advances in the operationalisation of the management plan.

This may mean that the organisational structure in the area of planning, monitoring and evaluation has become insufficient as a platform for the operationalisation of the Judicial Branch Management Plan. By virtue of the fact that evaluation involves a strategic and decision-making level of intervention, it is necessary to review its necessary articulation with the management and administration of the judiciary in the pafs.

Analysis matrix 2

Guidelines	Interviews	Subcategories Built	Expert assessment
Transformation of the judicial management y its actors	E1: Management in terms of improving working conditions has been deficient. With the exception of the TSJ officials who do enjoy incentives and employment benefits in terms of food, health insurance, transport, etc. However, the officials who work in the Circuits have not been able to obtain the benefits they are entitled to. Judicial No (L:6O-67)	job satisfaction	Judicial Officer: Working conditions and benefits must be in line with the social and economic situation of the country.
	E2. Working groups and periodic meetings are held with the participation of the highest authorities involved in the justice system, and the demands proposed by each of them and the commitments acquired for the solution of the problems observed are recorded in the minutes. 165)	Institutional commitment, appreciation of democratic principles.	The existing The existing evaluation instruments are mostly are statistical data, there is a need to innovate.
	E3: I believe that there is a political will for technological transformation and this is evidenced by the change of office equipment and administrative materials, among them, in addition to their provision. constant over the last periods (L:57-6O)	Policies from Modernisation and technological transformation.	Judicial Management policies can be made more effective by increasing the the Investment in technological endowment y an advisory body for the Planning Directorate
	E4: The concerns and proposals of the actors in the justice system often remain on the table or on paper because they are not put into practice because there is a bureaucracy or there is no real and concrete will to solve these problems.	Effectiveness in the Processes of communication and stakeholder participation.	

Prepared by Montiel (2023)

Osuna et al. (2004). The success of programme management will depend, on the one hand, on the ability to define the strategy of action and, on the other hand, on the structures possessing adequate conditions to manage the complex internal activities of the organisation. Such an organisational structure should be aligned with the optimal resources, organisational culture and leadership process.

In this context, theorising about the transformation of judicial management and its actors as a category revealed by the study, involves understanding that structural changes are not immediate, and require the concurrence of a series of factors both internal and external, inherent to the organisational field, social, political and economic environment, as well as being oriented towards modernised, innovative and open to new management possibilities. In this process of implementation of the Judicial Strategic Plan for the period 2013-2019, expectations favourable to the transformation of judicial management were configured with various preeminent elements derived from the commitment to institutionality, appreciation of democratic principles, search for innovations in professional performance and willingness to improve the quality of judicial service, meanings that give strength to the institution.

As shown by the following accounts of key informants in relation to these favourable internal conditions and as evidenced by the following: "...I feel a personal satisfaction with the activation of academic activities aimed at judges and other administrative staff who are part of the Judiciary, as they have the possibility of developing study programmes through the National School of the Judiciary. In addition to - work incentives such as salary bonuses for those civil servants who obtain university degrees and specialisations". (E1:L:82-91)Likewise, this source of information expresses its perception of the changes in this way: "...I believe that modernisation is possible, as evidenced by the authorisation for the holding of hearings by telematic means. This modality undoubtedly brings benefits on a large scale, generating procedural speed and simplifying judicial processes, since complex situations can be resolved". (E1:L:101- 108) Regarding these internal strengths, informant 3, agrees with the conditionsfavourable in this way: "...I believe that there is a political will for technological transformation and this is evidenced by the change of office equipment and administrative materials, among them, in addition to their constant provision in recent periods." (E3:L:66-70) For his part, witness 2 exemplifies the effective response capacity of the institution in the context of the pandemic, referring to the positive impacts that the transformation of judicial management has achieved: "In the last decade, we can say without doubt that one of the situations that marked the development of judicial policies was the global pandemic of Covid 19, since our nation establishes as a constitutional guarantee that justice must be imparted without delays, without being paralysed and without procedural delays, which led those in charge of the justice system to implement new policies not yet applied in the country, This led those in charge of the justice system to implement new policies, not yet applied in the country, concerning the use of technology under the application of telematic hearings, the implementation of internet and special electronic equipment in court, prisons, prosecutors and public defence offices, in order to impart justice despite the time that made oral hearings impossible, i.e. those that could only be held in the presence of the parties to the proceedings.This policy, which brought about the modernisation of the judicial system, shortening distances and times through technology, is still in place today, obtaining satisfactory results in terms of shortening times in those trials which, due to distance or complexities in transport and transfers, were not possible to carry out in less time, contributing to a more expeditious justice in those specific cases" (E2:L:32-56).However, realities are perceived according to the location from which they are observed, in this sense, these internal conditions also have meanings that show the weaknesses of management, in this regard, this subject expresses that: It should be noted that the Judiciary is indebted to modernisation and investment in the updating and implementation of technology, systems and computer equipment that would allow for efficient and much more expeditious judicial action. There is a high shortage of electronic means in the Courts at the national level, which is contrary to Strategic Objective 1.1 of the Strategic Plan, specifically the provisions of 1.1.8, 1.1.9, 1.1.10, and 1.1.11. There has been no implementation of a single system for monitoring cases, nor has a permanent system of statistics been set up to verify jurisdictional performance and other indicators of national and international relevance, and there is no evidence of the necessary investment to cover the requirements and needs of the Courts. (E1: L:29-46). Similarly, it states that "...Management in terms of improving working conditions has been deficient. With the exception of the TSJ officials who do enjoy incentives and employment benefits in terms of food, health insurance, transport, etc. However, the officials who provide services in the judicial circuits do not (E1: L:60-67).

According to this interviewee, "...the creation of competitive examinations for judges and prosecutors, the creation of administrative and public management support offices for the justice system, the provision of resources for the modernisation and humanisation of judicial facilities, improvements in the salaries of justice system employees...". (E2: L:197-202). Understanding that these unresolved situations affect the efficiency of judicial governance. According to Binder (2004), the weakness of the judiciary in the continent is, in turn, a problem for political systems and democracies, and he therefore proposes overcoming reductionist visions of the construct of "judicial government" and taking it up again as a mechanism for moving towards judicial independence and the consolidation of the democratic system.

In synthesis, it can be inferred that the search for the transformation of judicial management and its actors is based on the understanding that the institutional framework alone will not be transformed, but will depend on the thinking and instruments used in the process of modernisation and structural change. According to this analysis, the strategies contemplated in the Strategic Plan relating to the consolidation of the technological infrastructure, interconnection of the headquarters of the judiciary, provision of equipment and technological innovation, digitalisation projects, among others, have not been effectively achieved, placing the effectiveness and efficiency of management in an unfavourable perception.

Analysis matrix 3

Guidelines	Interviews	Subcategories Built	Expert assessment
	E1: The approach plans in the	Effective linkage	Civil servant
	pre-trial detention centres and	judicial policy	Judicial:
	detention centres, the following emerged	with other branches of the	Consistency of the
	as a support mechanism for	public authority.	Public policy and
	part of the judiciary before the		strengthening the
	Inefficiency of other powers		institutionalism of the
	Managers of system by		Status.
Democratisation of the judiciary.	for example the penitentiary, in guaranteeing the democratic justice system (L:137-143).		
	E2. No knowledge of the application of user surveys (L: 171-172).	Insufficient user liaison mechanisms user liaison mechanisms	
	E3: The implementation of technological tools for the purpose of user/citizen access in order to safeguard their rights and thus guaranteeing their rights. also the constitutional ones (L:26- 28)	Capacity respon siveness to new social demands	Judicial Management policies can be made more effective by increasing the the Investment in technological endowment y an advisory body in the Planning Directorate
	E4: I believe that this democratisation of the system is very slow, and the conditions for it to progress do not exist either. (E: 26-36)		

Prepared by Montiel (2023)

As for the category: Democratisation of the judiciary, defined according to the purpose of identifying the structures of democratic, participatory relations established in the strategic plan of the judiciary with an impact on the quality of its management. The analysis revealed that the participation of the actors is conditioned by the evaluation and performance mechanisms internal to the organisation, and by the inherent function of the positions in the organisational structure of the judiciary established in the Organic Law of the Supreme Court of Justice (2004).With argument in the following account; "...No mechanisms have been implemented for the purpose of receiving concerns, proposals, opinions, comments, among others for the purpose of administrative improvement and to be guarantors of user or citizen access for the necessary administrative structural change to achieve greater effectiveness and efficiency". (E3: L:75-83).Regarding the participation of civil society, this witness states; "I am not aware of the application of user consultation instruments" (e2: l:170-172). (E2: L:170-172) In order to understand the scope of democratisation, we analyse below what is established in the Constitution of the Bolivarian Republic of Venezuela, the Plan for the Homeland and the Strategic Plan of the Judiciary for the period 2013-2019 on Democracy and participation.

Democracy Analysis Matrix

Plan for the Homeland 2013-2019	Judicial Branch Strategic Plan 2013-2019 Axis 1: Objective 1	Constitution RBV 1999 Participatory Democracy
Consolidating and expanding power and socialist democracy.	Optimise the conditions for guaranteeing access to justice, the right of access to	The state is conceived as democratic and participatory, in
Achieving full sovereignty as a	effective judicial protection and due process	in which civil society forms
irrervesible project guarantee	process for the protection of the rights of the	Part active part of development
Bolivarian,	national, collective interests,	social. Comportando a
	as well as raising the dignity and	management transformation
	personality development in	Public a from at
	A society democratic society,	citizen participation in the
	participatory and proactive.	social programmes and policies,
		becoming a spokesperson for
		needs and control
		social management.

Prepared by Montiel (2023)

According to the subcategories defined on the basis of the discourses and narratives, compared in turn with what is constitutionally established on Democracy and the participation of the actors, it is interpreted that there is no conjunction between what is constitutionally established with the strategies and objectives of the general plans of the Nation and the Strategic Plan of the Judiciary respectively, or at least that is how the informants perceive it, which could be configuring elements that hinder the exercise of participatory democracy and therefore the scope of the necessary democratisation of justice in the country. The Venezuelan political system has undergone a great transformation from the point of view of participation, starting with the provisions of the nation's political charter, oriented towards a participatory and protagonist democracy, which constitutes the current basis of society and democratic institutions, It is precisely at this point where the transformations announced in judicial management enable full access to justice, effective judicial protection and due process, and are therefore ways of achieving the democratisation of justice and the paradigm of Open Justice. It is therefore important to review the structures that guide judicial management in order to resize, make decisions and implement the necessary modifications.

4.3. Third Moment: What to do

4.3.1. Categorical Synopsis

By way of illustration, the configuration of the concepts inherent in the implementation process.

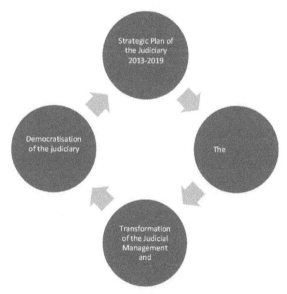

Prepared by Montiel (2023)

PROPOSAL

Monitoring and evaluation model to strengthen the management of the Strategic Plan of the Judiciary in Venezuela.

Rationale:

The judicial system in Venezuela needs to design and implement a monitoring and evaluation model to improve the management of the Strategic Plan of the Judiciary, with an integral vision of the critical knots at the cognitive, political, cultural, participatory and transforming level of the old structures, based on Strategic Planning and new forms of effective governance, I therefore propose to review the paradigm of Open Justice for its implementation in the country as a way to discuss and execute public policies based on evidence that will improve the results achieved, increase levels of trust and improve the relationship between justice and society.

GENERAL GUIDELINES

1. Link the Executive Directorate of the Judiciary and its regional offices to the strategic vision of the monitoring and evaluation model.

2. Articulate the Strategic Planning with the systematic evaluation process, defining short and medium term objectives.

3. Identify strategies and goals in a time frame, with the necessary resources for their development.

4. Establish the procedure, techniques and instruments for the execution of the Strategic Plan, specifying the programmes, projects, goals, management indicators, responsible parties, budgets and schedule of activities.

5. Coordinate a monitoring and follow-up system for the Strategic Plan.

6. Disserïve an operational model (mapping) to distinguish available resources in terms of budget, human talent and organisational structure against beneficiary impact.

CONCLUSIONS

In congruence with the purposes of this analysis, it is important to highlight that Venezuela is consolidated on the basis of the Constitution of the Bolivarian Republic of Venezuela. Venezuela (1999), in a democratic and social State of law and justice which upholds life, liberty, equality, democracy, solidarity, social responsibility and, in general, the pre-eminence of human rights as the supreme values of its legal system, ethics and political pluralism, elements that make up the socio-political context of the nation and to which judicial management, democratic institutions and citizenship are circumscribed, the latter being configured not only in the social fabric but also in the framework of relations with the State.With regard to the purpose of characterising the management of the judiciary in Venezuela from the perspective of the actors involved, it is concluded that it is necessary to improve the quality of judicial management, extending the processes of modernisation and technological innovation, with the provision of equipment to all judicial circuits, as well as extending the coverage of benefits and employment incentives for civil servants in the system. It is also imperative to review the administrative structures, management of positions and the legal framework in this area.In order to identify the democratic and participatory structures established in the Strategic Plan with an impact on the quality of their management. The absence of effective mechanisms to promote participation and democratise justice was found, a situation that hinders compliance with the strategic guidelines of the Nation, in addition to the actions of the Strategic Plan of the Judiciary and what is constitutionally conceived. According to the purpose of establishing theoretical and methodological contributions on the evaluation of the strategic plan of the judiciary in Venezuela. It is interpreted that in the implementation of judicial policies, there is a lack of monitoring, control of their execution and investment of inputs. It is therefore concluded that there is a need to develop a monitoring and evaluation model to strengthen the management of the Strategic Plan of the judiciary in Venezuela.The future of the justice service lies in designing and implementing evidence-based public policies that improve outcomes, increase levels of trust and improve the relationship between justice and society. To create this link in which justice back to the central place it should occupy in a democratic community, I propose to review the Open Justice paradigm for its implementation in our country.

BIBLIOGRAPHICAL REFERENCES

Arellano G. (2014). introduction: La enserïanza de la evaluación de Polfác6n Pûblicas.
In A. R. Cazares, La evaluaci6n de Polfticas pûblicas en América Latina: métodos y propuestas docentes (p. 7). Mexico: CIDE-Centro CLEAR para América Latina-Red Inter-Americana de Educaci6n en Administraci6n Pûblica .
ASAMBLEA NACIONAL CONSTITUYENTE (1999). Constitution of the Bolivarian Republic of Venezuela. Caracas, Venezuela. Gaceta Oficial de la República Bolivariana de Venezuela No. 5.453 Extraordinario. 24/03/2000. Amendment No. 1 to the Constitution of the Bolivarian Republic of Venezuela.

Binder, Alberto (2006). Gobierno Judicial y democratici6n de la Justicia. In Sistemas Judiciales. Arïo 5, No 10. Justice Studies Center of the Americas. Buenos Aires.

Cansino, Cesar (2008) La Muerte de la Ciencia Polftica. Editorial Sudamericana. Buenos Aires.
Osuna, José & Marquez, Carolina (2004) Guia para la evaluaci6n de Politicas Pûblicas. Instituto de Desarrrollo Regional. Fundaci6n Universitaria. Spain.

Oszlak, Oscar & O'Donnell, Guillermo (1981) Estado y polfticas estatales en América Latina: Hacia una estrategia de investigación. Centro de Estudios de Estado y Sociedad (CEDES). Buenos Aires.
Sartori, Giovanni (1992) La Polftica, L6gica Y Método en las Ciencias Sociales. Fondo de Cultura Econ6mica. México.

Taylor, S. and Bodgan, R. (1992) Introduction to qualitative research methods.

Paidos. Barcelona. Esparïa.

Vilas Carlos (2011) Despues del Neoliberalismo: Estado y Procesos Politicos en América Laitina. Colecci6n Planificaci6n y Politicas Pûblicas. Ediciones Universidad Nacional Lanus.

Documents:

Bolivarian Republic of Venezuela. Supreme Court of Justice (2015) Lfíneas Generales del Plan Estratégico del Poder Judicial 2013-2019.

ECLAC (2019) Social Panorama of Latin America. Edici6n 2019.

Ministry of Territorial Policy and Public Administration. Agencia Estatal de Evaluaci6n de las Politicas Pûblicas y la Calidad de los Servicios (2010). Fundamentos de Evaluaci6n de las Politicas Pûblicas. Madrid, Spain.